NANTWICH

ANDREW LAMBERTON & ANNE WHEELER

The History Press

This book is dedicated to Margaret and the late Mabel Wooldridge,
who have both been keen supporters of Nantwich Museum for many years.

***

Proceeds from the sale of this book go to Nantwich Museum.
By buying this book you are supporting the work of the museum.

Nantwich Museum

Pillory Street, Nantwich, Cheshire, CW5 5BQ
tel: 01270 627104 www.nantwichmuseum.org.uk

First published 2012

The History Press
The Mill, Brimscombe Port
Stroud, Gloucestershire, GL5 2QG
www.thehistorypress.co.uk

isbn 978 0 7524 5830 4

Typesetting and origination by The History Press
Printed in Great Britain

CONTENTS

ACKNOWLEDGEMENTS

The authors would like to express their gratitude to all those who have contributed to this publication. Without the support of numerous individuals this book would not have been possible and we are grateful to everyone who has helped in any way. We would like to thank the Board of Management of Nantwich Museum for supporting the project and all those — of which there are far too many to name individually — who have contributed photographs to the collections of Nantwich Museum over the years. Without the generosity of these individuals and organisations the museum would not have had such a rich collection on which to draw.

Special thanks is given to all those members of the Polish community who responded to an appeal for photographs and information for an exhibition at the museum in 2010. Prior to this, the museum had no images or first-hand memories of the Polish Resettlement Camp at Doddington, and this represented a notable gap in the collection. Thanks to the generosity of those who provided photographs and memories, this gap has been filled and the camp is now represented in the museum's collections and in the local and social history of the area.

Our grateful thanks go to Graham Dodd, who has been of enormous help and support throughout the project, particularly with scanning images.

Thanks also to Fiona Swain, the Museum's Administration Assistant, who has been helpful throughout and to Sarah Hannay, who has assisted through the inputting of the catalogue of negatives onto the computer database.

Finally, we wish to acknowledge the help and support of Zosia Biegus, Jan Czerski, Kate Dobson (Community Learning Officer), Barbara Fisher, Angela Graham (Business Development Manager from October 2011 to January 2012), Pauline Roach, Muriel Shakeshaft and Jane Stevenson.

INTRODUCTION

This book brings to publication for the first time a selection of photographs of Nantwich and the surrounding area exclusively from the collection of Nantwich Museum. The museum's collection has been built up over more than thirty years and includes pictures taken by both professional and amateur photographers. Many of the images in this book are from photographs which have been donated by private individuals, and the original photographs have been accessioned into the museum's formal collection. Other photographs have been loaned to the museum for copying and the originals returned to the owner. More recently, digital images have been sent to the museum electronically and these have been stored both on the computer and as hard copies. The museum is grateful to everyone who has contributed images to the photographic collection in any way.

The images in this book have arrived at the museum in all sorts of ways over the years and, as a result, the amount of information we have about them varies enormously. Sometimes photographs arrive at the museum with little or no supporting information – proving quite a challenge to those tasked with the responsibility of cataloguing them. It often takes quite a bit of research and detective work to uncover the story behind the image. Sometimes a wonderful story will reveal itself and, at other times, it will only be possible to find a location and estimate a date. Sadly, some photographs prove impossible to identify and remain, for the time being at least, a mystery. This only highlights the importance of recording as much information as possible whenever the opportunity presents itself.

The process of compiling this book has enabled the authors to assess the museum's photographic collection and to undertake research, which adds to our understanding of the image and the social and local history that it illustrates. It has also provided the impetus for digitising the collection so that images can be made more readily accessible. One of the other advantages of digital images is the ability to zoom right into the picture and study small, but often crucial, details, which can help with dating and identification and bring new information to light. The museum is currently copying all the photographic images in the collection to digital format so that members of the public will have the opportunity of easier access to these through the museum website. It will also make it easier for the museum to display these images from time to time in future exhibitions.

When I took up the position of Curator of Nantwich Museum in October 2008, I was pleasantly surprised at the size and quality of the photographic collection. Having worked with photographic collections at other museums, I particularly value photographs as a social record and appreciate their potential to enhance our understanding of the local area and of the past. Photographs have an immediacy and accessibility which is hard to beat, and help bring the past alive. This book aims to showcase a sample of the rich and varied history of the Nantwich area during the nineteenth and twentieth centuries.

For this book, Andrew and I have enjoyed selecting over 190 images from a large and fascinating collection. We have sought to represent a range of aspects of the area's vibrant history through the inclusion of topographical views, postcards, portraits, publicity shots, official photographs and family snaps. We have tried to focus on quality images which are not widely known and have never been published before. It is hoped that this book will contain at least some information and pictures which are new to even the most dedicated of Nantwich scholars.

Nantwich is fortunate in having a wealth of photogenic buildings and views, and, while we have included several undoubtedly 'pretty pictures' such as views of the river and attractive timber-framed buildings, we have also included some less picturesque images including scenes of dereliction and demolition. The pleasant and genteel aspects of life in an attractive and affluent market town are reflected in views of the opulent Brine Baths Hotel and the magnificent Parkfield House, which was home to the famous cricketer A.N. Hornby. A reminder of a less pleasant aspect of life in pre-1970s Nantwich is provided through images of the tannery, which was responsible for creating an objectionable smell in the air.

It is interesting to see buildings that have since been demolished alongside those which have survived through the centuries and look much the same to this day. Shops that have long gone reflect changing lifestyles and fashions. Factories which were once the lifeblood of the town and provided steady employment for many local families have been bulldozed to make way for new housing. Similarly, farms and green fields have disappeared beneath modern estates as the town has grown.

History is all about change and continuity and photographs are a wonderful means of capturing this. It is often the most ordinary, everyday scene that is the most interesting, just as it is often the background details and 'incidentals' that reveal the most. Nantwich is changing all the time and today's photographs are tomorrow's history. Over the last thirty years Nantwich Museum has been actively recording and collecting the history of the town and it hopes to be able to continue doing so well into the future. If you have any photographs relating to Nantwich that you are willing to donate or lend for copying, then Nantwich Museum will be delighted to hear from you.

Anne Wheeler, 2012

Anne Wheeler.

Andrew Lamberton with museum staff. Clockwise from top left: Angela Graham, Kate Dobson, Fiona Swain.

1

TOWN CENTRE

One of the earliest photographs from the museum's collection, this rare image shows the group of five shops which stood on an island site in the middle of Nantwich Square immediately prior to demolition in 1872. A close examination shows the boarded-up shop windows. One wonders what the people are doing there. On the extreme right can be seen the typically Victorian double-fronted bow windows of the shop of Edward Hounsum Griffiths, printer, bookseller and stationer.

The Queen's Aid House at No. 41 High Street on the Square, taken around 1880 and showing the grocery shop of William Sandford. There is a large Royal Exchange advertisement between the second floor windows, where the Queen's Aid Board is now. Advertisements for Huntley and Palmers biscuits and Colman's Mustard can be seen in the windows. Both businesses are still in existence. Note the entries on either side of the shop (numerous in old Nantwich) and the large pile of rubble on the left.

Left: A horse is held patiently by a young boy while its owner visits the shop of William and Mary Lovatt, tailor, milliner and woollen drapers, at No. 46 High Street, *c.* 1890. Rows of striped socks can be seen hanging in the window. The sag in the middle of the shop frontage is due to subsidence and can already be seen in the upper storeys. It is more pronounced today, at the frontage of Nantwich Bookshop.

Below: Henry Bowker's shop, *c.* 1890. The shop was in Churchyardside, close to the Market Hall, and Henry Bowker was the local photographer for the town. Most, if not all of the previous photographs shown in this book were taken by him. He was also a picture framer and stationer, having a shop in Hospital Street before moving to Churhyardside in 1865. He was here until just after 1890. Note the church graveyard railings, the trees and unfinished laying of the kerbstones. The family with the empty cart may well have been to the market.

The Square, *c.* 1890. Note the granite setts and a horse and two-wheeled coach. Behind are the iron railings surrounding the consecrated ground of St Mary's parish church graveyard, with an abundance of trees. To the right, at No. 37 High Street, is Alfred Hill's printer and stationers shop, with the Printing Office sign in large letters. A nearby gas lamp completes the scene.

A postcard from the Edwardian era showing Nantwich Square, *c.* 1907. Although a cart can be seen, bicycles are much in evidence. W.H. Smith have recently taken over Alfred Hill's shop, although the large Printing Office Board remains. Just beyond, Lawtons the drapers is festooned with sale signs and straw boaters can be seen. In the distance, P.H. Chesters' grocery shop is still there, showing how narrow the Pillory Street end was in those days. Large posters adorn Youngs the Chemists shop on the corner of Mill Street, and George Bros, ironmongers and cycle agents, have taken over the shop of William Lovatt. On the extreme right are Amies boot and shoe shop and Furnivals, grocer and wine merchant.

Above: W.H. Smith & Sons shop at No. 37 High Street. The modern (in those days) gas lamp shows up clearly against the ivy-covered side of the building. There are railings on this side and the bollards at the end of Church Walk are clearly visible. Smiths is now selling artists' materials and leather goods as well as being a newsagents, stationers and booksellers. The Printing Office sign has now gone. The little girl with the dog cuts a forlorn figure in contrast to the group of boys, one of whom wears a large apron suggesting that he is an errand boy. Note the entry door on the right.

Right: An atmospheric scene showing Church Walk, *c.* 1910. In the distance is the west end of St Mary's parish church, known by some as 'The Cathedral of South Cheshire'. The church has served the town for nine centuries as the centre for religious worship. It was, however, also used to house prisoners after the Battle of Nantwich in 1644. Its unusual octagonal tower rises high above the town, the top of which is said to be on a level with the base of nearby Acton church tower. Iron railings line each side of the cobbled walk and the ivy is in abundance on the side of W.H. Smith's shop.

A busy scene in Churchyardside, *c.* 1920. This photograph shows workmen relaying granite setts outside the market hall entrance. Behind them on the right is the shop of William Berry, photographer and picture framer, who took over from Henry Bowker in the early 1890s. As was typical of the time, blinds are drawn over the shop windows to protect against the sun.

Parr's Bank, No. 34 High Street, *c.* 1910. The architecture of the building is described as Edwardian Baroque and this branch of the bank was opened around 1902. Parr's Bank was established in Warrington in 1788; by 1900 it had 136 branches and by 1918, 329 branches. It was taken over by Westminster Bank in 1923. It stood until the late 1970s when it was demolished and replaced with a modern building, which is now the current premises for NatWest Bank plc. The windows on the second floor display 'Offices to Let' signs. The Manager of Parr's Bank in 1913 is listed as Mr A.O. Coppack. Next door is Mr Poole, a well-known watchmaker and jeweller.

Stretch & Harlock's shop, 1920. This shop was formed from the partnership of two Nantwich Quaker families. One of Nantwich's most iconic shop fronts, this shop has been a landmark building on the Square since it was built in 1850. Occupying a large corner plot, it has provided Nantwich folk with all kinds of material for over 120 years. It sold ladies' fashions, household linens and soft furnishings. They also had a men's tailoring and outfitting department, and a funeral business in a nearby premises on the corner of Pepper Street. The young men gathered outside the shop doorway are shop assistants, judging by their smart attire.

Motor cars in Nantwich Square, c. 1925. This is the first photograph we have of cars (all with soft tops) parked at right angles to the kerb by the new War Memorial. W.H. Smith's has now had its pseudo-Tudor makeover and an early Crosville bus waits for passengers at the bus stop. Ladies in fashionable cloche hats stand behind the vehicles. In the distance can just be seen the cupola of the new store of P.H. Chesters, and the wider Pillory Street end is noticeable. On the extreme right is the grocer's shop of W.H. Grocott & Son.

Nantwich War Memorial, *c.* 1925. It was unveiled and dedicated in 1921 by General Sir Beavoir de Lisle, Commander-in-Chief of the Western Division. Constructed of Darley Dale stone, it was designed by P.H. Lockwood of Chester. Its pristine colour stands out against the background but has since weathered well over the intervening years. The names of 125 Nantwich men who were killed in action during the First World War are inscribed around the base, to which have been added forty-three names after the Second World War. The many wreaths surrounding the memorial underline the feelings of Nantwich people for those who gave their lives so that we might live.

The Square, *c.* 1935. The cars in this later photograph now mainly have a hard roof and there is a white line painted on the roadway showing where cars are allowed to park. A group of children wait to go home after school. Bicycles can be seen on both sides of the Square. In the distance, a traffic light stands at the corner of Hospital Street and the Square. F.W. Woolworth's has now arrived on the Square – on the extreme right.

The Square, *c.* 1925. Old cars are parked here, all have soft tops, some folded down, mudguards, running boards and the external spare wheel on the side. Bowens the drapers have an agent's sign for Pullars of Perth, and at the Queen's Aid House is the Queen Bess Café.

A Civil Defence exercise on the Square in 1941, demonstrating the use of gas masks, respirators and full protective clothing. The threat of chemical warfare during the early stages of the Second World War was very real and gas masks were readily issued. The parents of author Andrew Lamberton married in Leeds in 1939 and had their gas masks with them on their wedding day!

Nantwich Square, *c.* 1970. The iron railings surrounding the church graveyard have now gone, probably a victim of the war effort. On the left is the Old Vaults, known locally as 'the Potting Shed', while across Castle Street is Vernon Cooper's electrical shop. Vernon Cooper was a well-known figure in the town. A motor-racing enthusiast, in the 1950s and '60s he regularly competed in the Monte Carlo Rally. Next is Grices the Chemists, Craft Cleaners and Chatwins (the local bakery) with its tearoom upstairs. George Mason took over the former Woolworths shop after it moved to the new Swine Market site in the mid-1960s. On the extreme right is the National Westminster Bank, still using the original Parr's Bank building.

Shops in High Street looking from the Hospital Street end towards the Square, *c.* 1970. Youngs the Chemists (on the right) was one of three shops. This one sold chinaware but is now empty – posters in the shop window advertise Hoffman's Circus and a motocross race at Bickerton. Next, on the corner, is G.F. & A. Brown, wine and spirit merchants, then another shop belonging to Youngs, selling veterinary and pet supplies. The tall building behind is Leas the ironmongers. Strangely, Nantwich people have always pronounced the name 'Leas' to rhyme with 'shears', as if there was an 'r' in the name, which there isn't!

High Street, *c.* 1971. Not long after the previous photograph was taken, the corner shop of Youngs the chemists at the Hospital Street end was demolished. This shows the demolition in progress. The writing on the front of the lorry reads Five Towns Demolition and obviously refers to the five towns in the nearby Potteries. St Mary's parish church tower and roof of the south transept is in the distance, and the end of the Lamb Hotel behind the demolition crane.

2

SURROUNDING AREA

Carrington's hat shop, *c.* 1870. This hatter's shop was run by 70-year-old Mary Carrington, of No. 13 High Street, and was located on the corner of Oat Market at the base of the Oat Market/Swine Market island site. Note the bars on the window to the left of the shop doorway and the cobbled streets. Next door is James Hulse's saddler's shop. To the right is a rare view looking along Oat Market to the Red Lion (the tall building at the far end), and in between, the two-storey building is the rear of the Nantwich Arms public house.

Porch House, No. 64b Welsh Row, *c.* 1900. This house was built on the site of an earlier Porch House, hence its name. Around 1875, it was a boarding school for boys run by an aged Wesleyan Methodist called Mr Orchard. It had accommodation for twenty boys and they also took a few day pupils. Between around 1890 and 1913 it was a girls' school run by Mrs Alice Prince. It was later owned by well-known Nantwich man, Bill Schofield.

Opposite above: The Brine Baths Hotel, *c.* 1925. This photograph shows the original building, to which has been added extensions in a lighter coloured material to both of its sides. The hotel was opened in 1883 and later on had as many as fifty-four bedrooms. It was intended to provide medicinal baths using brine pumped up locally, but it never really achieved its aim of being a spa. It did, however, become a centre for the hunting fraternity of South Cheshire and a luxury hotel.

Opposite below: The Dining Room at the Brine Baths Hotel, *c.* 1930. This photograph illustrates the elegance of the upmarket hotel between the wars. On average, there was a maximum of thirty permanent residents at the hotel. All the guests knew each other and it was just like one big country house party.

DINING ROOM - BRINE BATHS HOTEL - NANTWICH.

Hospital Street, *c.* 1920. This picture clearly shows the granite setts on the road and the shop selling Rabau Belgian lace on the corner of Church Lane. In the distance is a sign for the Victoria Temperance Hotel (The Cocoa House), offering accommodation to cyclists. In the foreground,

on the right, is Frederick Ankers' antique and furniture shop, Clifford Hassall's Clifton Café, the sweet shop of Charles Foster, who made his own toffee and was known as 'Toffee Joe', and finally Sherratt's shop on the extreme right.

A rare photograph of Parkfield House off Wellington Road, taken by William Berry, *c.* 1910. This was the home of the famous cricketer Albert Hornby. He captained the England cricket team against Australia in 1882, which led to the Ashes being introduced to the cricketing world shortly afterwards. Note the large sun canopy over the front door and the large conservatory on the side. As Albert had four sons, the little girl just might be his granddaughter, Georgina.

Opposite above: The Dining Room at the Miners' Convalescence Home, *c.* 1950. The contrast to the photograph on page 23 couldn't be more pronounced. The opulence is gone and been replaced with a more austere and almost soulless ambience. The same fireplace is seen, but from the opposite side. There are different lights and a minimum of china on view. The difference between the hotel and the convalescent home couldn't be more marked.

Opposite below: Pillory Street, *c.* 1940. At the far end of the picture, at No.16 Pillory Street, is Sterlings boot and shoe shop, then comes Lightfoots the saddler, Lucy Peake the baker, and Owens the pork butcher. The K Shoes sign hangs over Talbots shoe shop, then Hunters the grocers with its name on the sun blind, and W.J. Green's fish shop. In High Street are Ferry's the tailors and, finally, Young's the chemists.

Elm House, Pillory Street, *c.* 1959. A photograph of the frontage of Elm House has proved elusive for a long, long time. Happily, Nantwich Museum now has this one, taken from a slide. Built by George Cappur, cheese-factor, in 1788 on the site of Maisterson's moated Hall, it has an unusual and distinctive semi-circular inset above the front door. Among its occupants have been P.H. Chesters, the grocer, and Samuel Sproston, a local man who married Miss de Trafford, a wealthy lady who donated the land by the railway to the Catholic Church, on which St Anne's Church was built. Finally, Haighton's the dentist had a surgery here prior to its demolition around 1960.

Mill Street, 1961. Continuing on from the Pillory Street photograph but some twenty-one years later, Youngs the chemists are on the corner of High Street and Mill Street. Note the road signs to Crewe and the Potteries. Looking down Mill Street, the Bedford van is parked outside Schofield's butcher shop. The Wickstead Arms can just be seen beyond. On the corner of Barker Street is G. & W. Lea the ironmongers. Across Mill Street is Mathers the cabinet maker, the Nantwich Guardian Office, and then, finally, Thomas Daniels the tobacconist on the corner of High Street.

Swinemarket/Oatmarket, *c.* 1962. This view, looking north from the bend in High Street, shows the newly cleared site of a group of houses and shops which occupied the small piece of ground between Swinemarket and Oatmarket. As well as several shops, it had two public houses. The buildings on the left in Swinemarket survived a few more years before they too were demolished.

Nantwich Mill, *c.* 1965. A peaceful and well-known picture taken from the town bridge. To the left is Bower's Row, built to house workers at the cotton mill. These were demolished around 1970. The mill has a long history going back to 1228. After grinding corn for the locality for some 500 years, it became a cotton mill in 1798. This eventually closed down in 1874 and it reverted to a corn mill. Later, in the 1950s, it became Boughey's Mill and then a billiard hall. A catastrophic fire destroyed the mill in 1970 and it had to be demolished.

Basin End, *c.* 1965. Two boys are enjoying a spot of fishing at the canal side. The Shropshire Union Canal was built from Chester to Nantwich and opened in 1779. Its terminus was Basin End, Nantwich. It was not until 1835 that the southern link to Birmingham was cut. During this period much transport of goods, particularly cheese, was moved by water. The arrival of the railway in the 1840s and '50s proved a big blow to this method of transport, from which it never recovered. Nowadays, the canals have been revitalised with the impact of leisure and tourism.

The gas works, 1969. Formed in 1832, the works was situated off St Anne's Lane and provided the town with gas for around 150 years. Since demolition in the 1970s the site has been used as a car park. Concerns about toxic substances in the soil have meant delays in the development of this site.

The Technical Institute, Beam Street, 1969. Purpose-built in 1902 of red Ruabon brick, the Institute provided educational classes to teenagers and adults of Nantwich and the surrounding district for almost seventy years. It was also used by many local organisations for meetings and leisure activities. It was the building where school meals were eaten by Manor Road and Market Street schoolchildren in the 1940s and '50s. It was demolished soon after this photograph was taken. Nantwich Library now stands on the site.

Sir Edmund Wright almshouses on their original site in London Road, 1970. These almshouses were built in 1638 by Sir Edmund Wright (who became Lord Mayor of London in 1641) for six almsmen of the town. Priority was given to any man with the surname Wright. By 1975, the buildings had deteriorated to such an extent that the decision was made by the Trustees to dismantle, renovate and rebuild the almshouses next to the Sir John Crewe almshouses in Beam Street, where they stand today.

Left: The old Town Hall, *c.* 1971. It was rebuilt in 1868 after the foundations of the earlier building proved unsafe. It thereafter became a nineteenth-century centre for social and public events. In the early 1900s it was the hub of the town's entertainments; silent movies were seen by children on Saturday afternoons, who paid one penny on the ground floor or threepence in the red plush seats of the balcony.

Below: The old Town Hall stands in isolation immediately prior to demolition, *c.* 1971. It was built in 1858 and had a wide variety of uses over the intervening years, from public meetings, elections and theatre performances to lantern shows and dances. In 1945 it was considered unsafe for public use and was let to a motor accessories store. It was later taken over by Bill Spode as a DIY and timber store, but became empty in 1965 and was ultimately demolished in 1972. In the picture a board shows the goods entrance for W. Spode at the rear and to the right of this is Jack Field's motorcycle garage.

Natwest Bank and an empty shop in High Street, 1974. The bank occupies two buildings, separated by the empty shop vacated in 1972 by F.H. Burgess, engineering suppliers to the local farming industry. In the late 1970s, both this shop premises and and the Parr's Bank building on the right of the picture were demolished, to be replaced with a large, modern building.

The south side of Beam Street, 1974. This photograph shows the row of houses (now demolished) which stood between the end of Pepper Street and the end of Market Street. This row was typical of many of the older houses in the town which were not up to minimum housing standards of the modern day. The shop with the 'For Sale' sign may have been that of Maurice Smith, general outfitter.

The Co-op in Beam Street, 1978. This well-known Nantwich building has been around since about 1910 and many local people remember going there for their 'divi'. Fortunately, the building still stands and it now provides equipment for the elderly and infirm.

3

SHOPS

Hannah Hulmes stands outside her late husband Isaac's shop, No. 52 Hospital Street, *c.* 1891. To her right is possibly Ann Welch and in front of them both is Hannah's daughter, Milly, who became the mother of Freda Guest (*née* Gregory). Freda sang for many years in the 1950s with the Acton Operatic Society. There are advertisements in the window for Hudson's and Crosfield's soaps, twist tobacco and Peak Frean's Biscuits. The well-known local artist Herbert St John Jones lodged above the shop in the 1930s.

Above: Frederick Ankers' two shops at Nos 32 and 34 Hospital Street, *c.* 1901. Frederick was 73 years old when this photograph was taken and no doubt that is him standing in the shop doorway. His wife Ann stands outside the other shop. In 1865, he is described as a furniture broker and umbrella maker. In later years, he is still a furniture broker, but also a general dealer, as the shop windows indicate.

Left: The shop of James Sutton, tobacconist and stationer, No. 8 Pillory Street, *c.* 1913. He sold a variety of cigarettes and tobaccos, as can be seen in the window. Golden Dawn Cigarettes were particularly popular during the First World War. His was just one of several tobacconist shops in the town.

The Star Supply Stores in the High Street, opposite the Crown Hotel, mid-1930s. This was one of a national chain of grocery stores. Samples of different meats, ham and bacon, hang on hooks above the assistants' heads. Price labels in shillings and pence are much in evidence. There are adverts for Blue Seal Margarine.

One of a series of publicity photographs of the interior of P.H. Chesters' grocery shop at No. 6 Hospital Street, mid-1930s. There is no sign of any customers. The business had other shops in High Street and Pepper Street, and a delivery service that covered large parts of south Cheshire.

Above: The shop of G.A. Racklyeft, House Furnisher and Upholsterer, at No. 19 Pillory Street, *c.* 1950. Racklyeft had moved to larger premises from No. 45 High Street, and was listed in 1934 in Pillory Street and Queen Street, which is the cobbled street on the left-hand side of the photograph. Note the road sign for traffic turning left out of Love Lane.

Left: The Nantwich branch of F.W. Woolworth at No. 38 High Street, *c.* 1961. Woolworths came to Nantwich in the 1920s and stayed there until 1965, when it moved to the then new premises in Swinemarket. The store closed in 2009.

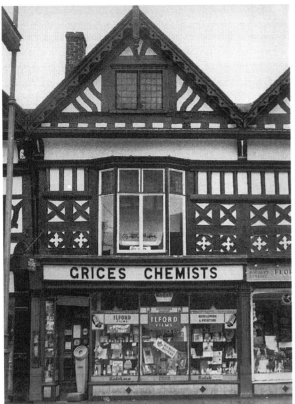

Grices the Chemists, No. 44 High Street, *c.* 1961. A long-established business, Joseph Grice was here in 1869. At the time of the photograph it was being run by the Stonelake family and the shop was renowned for its own patented hand cream. Their advertisement runs 'Always use Wyche Hand Cream. Unequalled for chapped or rough hands. Testimonials received from all parts of the country.'

The empty shop of Edward Ferry, No. 58 High Street, *c.* 1961. At the turn of the twentieth century, this was a thriving, bespoke tailoring business. On the top floor would be twelve tailors sitting cross-legged in the traditional manner and singing as they sewed. Long hours sitting on the floor with continual pressing against the knees made them somewhat bow-legged. Sometimes they would have to work 24 hours if a rush order came through, and a piece-work tailor earned just 25*s* a week.

Talbots shoe shop, No. 6 Pillory Street, *c.* 1961. The business was established in the early 1900s. By the 1950s Miss Norman was in charge and the shop specialised in high-class footwear, especially for children. In those days the latest trend here was an X-ray machine, which would show you how well a pair of new shoes fitted your feet. Toes showed up darkly against a green background. The business was taken over by Harry Corry in 1970, who sold it in 1989 when it moved to larger premises in Beam Street.

Ye Old Sweet Shoppe, No. 28 Pillory Street, *c.* 1961. A good photograph
of one of several sweet shops in the town. This one stands on the corner
of Love Lane. In 1938 it was run by Bessie Hughes and, at the time the
photograph was taken, by Doris Wright. In 1972 it was run by Mrs E.
Bridgewood. It is now a charity shop.

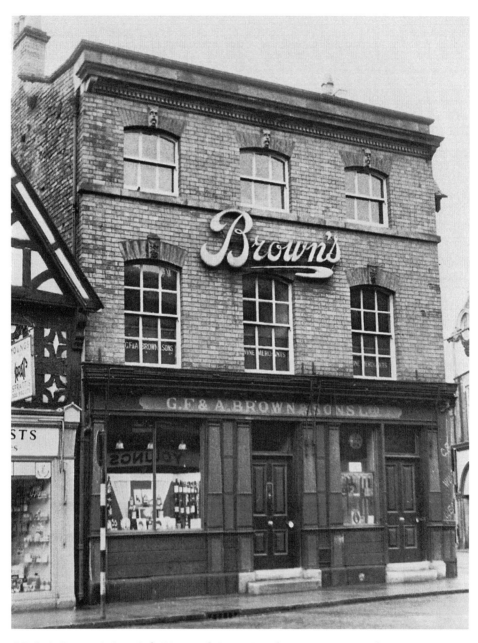

G.F. & A. Brown & Sons Ltd, Wine and Spirits Merchant at No. 47 High Street, *c*. 1961. Established some 100 years earlier, a wine merchants had been on these premises since 1841. George Frederick and Alfred were brothers. It ceased trading about 1969, was given a facelift shortly afterwards and is now the premises of HSBC Bank.

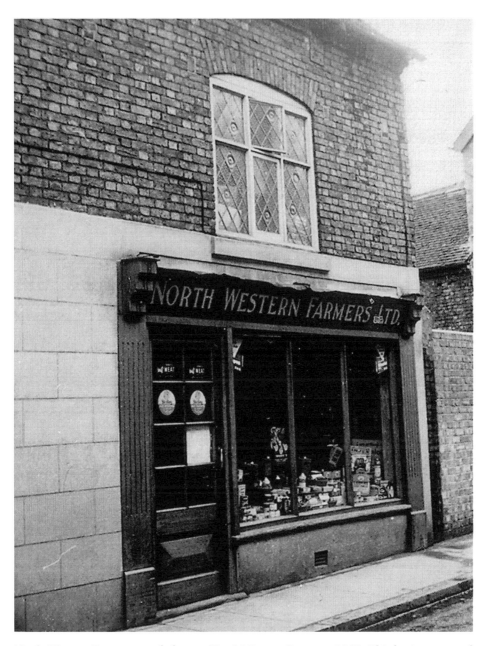

North Western Farmers retail shop at No. 14 Pepper Street, *c.* 1961. This business started out as a small local Farmers' Co-operative and has expanded over the intervening years. By the mid-1970s it had moved out to its present headquarters at Wardle.

Left: F.J. Mills', grocery shop at No. 25 High Street, *c.* 1961. Frederick James Mills ran the shop in 1914 and Elizabeth Mills in 1939. By 1964 it was empty. It is now the premises of the Britannia Building Society. It is a good example of a small, family-run business trying to compete against the big guns like P.H. Chesters and Stennett and Afford.

Below: The Zan Stores in temporary premises, Swine Market, *c.* 1961. The Zan Stores were previously at No. 13 High Street from the 1930s, until demolition of the whole block of buildings in 1959. They moved over to the buildings in the photograph but had to move out shortly after, when they too were demolished in 1963. The Zan Company was formed locally at Wheelock near Sandbach and sold general hardware, including cleaning materials, through their local stores.

Right: Melias the grocers at No.2 High Street, *c.* 1961. This shop stood on the corner of Waterlode. The company was established by Daniel Melia of Manchester in 1896. By the 1920s it had many branches in towns and cities in the north-west and Midlands. Some branches specialised in tea. The company packaged its own butter and sugar. The branch was here in the 1920s and closed in the mid-1960s, the building being demolished with the whole block in 1977.

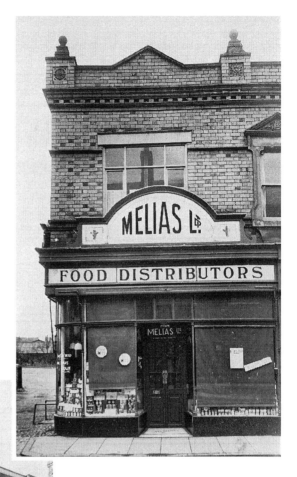

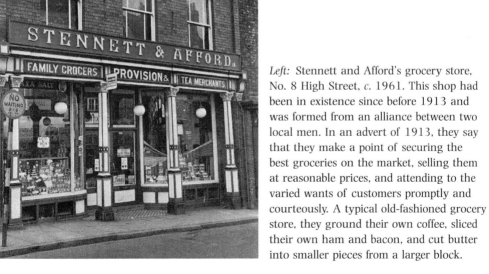

Left: Stennett and Afford's grocery store, No. 8 High Street, *c.* 1961. This shop had been in existence since before 1913 and was formed from an alliance between two local men. In an advert of 1913, they say that they make a point of securing the best groceries on the market, selling them at reasonable prices, and attending to the varied wants of customers promptly and courteously. A typical old-fashioned grocery store, they ground their own coffee, sliced their own ham and bacon, and cut butter into smaller pieces from a larger block.

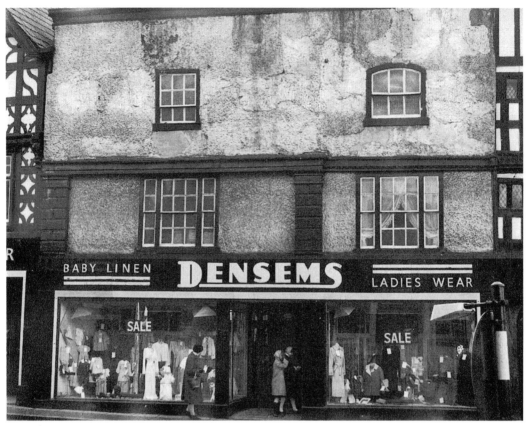

Above: Densems ladies and babywear shop, Nos 16 and 18 High Street, *c.* 1961. Already in operation in 1938, Densems became established as the major clothing retailer in the town. It was run by the Lake family, with John Lake in overall control. Next door was the menswear department and next to that was the children's and boys' wear department, managed by Bill Lake. At one time they also had a shop across the street. They stocked clothing made by the local clothing factories in the town.

Left: F.H. Burgess, ironmongers at No. 32 High Street, *c.* 1961. F.H. Burgess took over the ironmongers shop of Thomas Parsonage, and were operating from here by 1953. They sold hardware items to local farmers as well as to the general public. They moved out to larger premises in St Anne's Lane in 1972. Since then they have moved again to the Beam Heath Industrial Estate, off Middlewich Road – this site has now also closed. Note the road signs for the A51 pointing to Chester, Crewe and Whitchurch.

4

PUBS

The Three Pigeons at No. 20 Welsh Row, *c.* 1910. This is one of the oldest public houses in Nantwich, thought to have derived its name from the coat of arms of the Allen family of Brindley. The earliest recorded licensee was Samuel Bolis in 1765. When the Griffin Inn closed in High Street in 1801, its cockpit was moved here. At the far end of the building was a butcher's shop and the butcher used to sharpen his knife on the sandstone mounting block outside.

The Wickstead Arms, No. 11 Mill Street, 1920. This public house was named after the Wickstead family, who owned this and the adjacent property. By 1891 it was the property of Boddington's Brewery. Walter Bebbington was the licensee from 1910 to 1945. It had several previous names, including the Royal Oak, the Eagle and Child in 1787, and the Bluebell in 1791, before gaining its present name by 1822.

The Wickstead Arms, No. 11 Mill Street, c. 1961. This public house has now been replaced with a modern building. The Wickstead coat of arms is shown on the right. Beyond, on the left, is Schofield's the butcher, with a van parked outside. Note the 'No Entry' sign.

Left: The Union Vaults, No. 15 High Street, *c.* 1961. The Union Vaults opened as a public house in 1795 and its first licensee was John Lightfoot. Its name may well have come from the Act of Union, which came into force in 1801. In the 1880s it was known as Rayner's Vaults. Note the entry into the yard for stabling horses behind and the Maypole shop next door.

Below: The Gamecock, No. 2 Oatmarket, *c.* 1961. Although quite an old building, it only became a public house in 1928, when its licensee was Thomas Case. At the time this photograph was taken, the licensee was Jessie Betteley and it closed shortly after, in 1965. Note the double doors leading to a yard at the back. The Talbot pub is next door to the left and the Union Vaults to the right. It is now divided into two, with a shop on the ground floor and a restaurant above.

The Talbot, No. 6 Oatmarket, *c.* 1961. This public house was opened in 1796, with Charles Walker – who had previously kept the Talbot around the corner in Beam Street – as the licensee. In 1806 it was the property of Charles and Prussia Salmon and it had a yard and stable behind. It changed its name to Bowlers in 1989 and the Frog and Ferret in 1990. Thankfully, it has since reverted to its original name.

The White Lion, No. 7 Swinemarket, *c.* 1961. Its earliest recorded licensee was John Parkes in 1774, and the owner was Mr Rudyard. Its last licensee was William Ridgway in 1929, after which it became a private house. It was demolished with all the buildings in the picture shortly after the photograph was taken.

5

INDUSTRY

Charles Tilsley's shop at
No. 81 Hospital Street,
c. 1900. Shoemaking had
been a major business in
Nantwich since the sixteenth
century. It reached its peak
around 1879 but then
declined rapidly as the
manufacturing moved away
from being a family concern in
private houses to be replaced
by factory work. Charles
was one of the last of the
shoemaking families to have a
shop in the town. An advert
from about 1920 describes
him as a manufacturer of
every class of boots and shoes,
and states that hand-sewn
boots were made to measure.

Above: Joseph Willett's shop, Nos 5 and 6 Beam Street, *c.* 1910. Another well-known shoemaking family were the Willetts. They also had a shop in Pillory Street. As well as boots and shoes they made clogs on the Beam Street premises, and it is thought that George ('Clogger') Robinson took over the business here some time later. Clogs were popular with the working men around the beginning of the twentieth century. Samples of boots and shoes can be seen in the shop windows.

Left: The first in a series of atmospheric photographs from Harvey's Tannery in Millstone Lane, *c.* 1950. The man in the photograph is wearing protective gloves and apron. Animal hides were immersed in 8-foot deep pits for several weeks to loosen the flesh and animal hair in the tanning process. Traditionally a solution of oak bark was used but later on lime became popular. The most notable characteristic of a tannery, however, was the awful smell. Some readers may recall the overpowering stench of rotting animal flesh on that side of the town.

The beam house of Harvey's Tannery, *c.* 1950. The hides were suspended in the pits from a beam, to which they were tied. The pits contained varying strengths of solution and beamsmen transferred them from the weakest to the strongest solutions, as shown in this photograph.

The beam house of Harvey's Tannery, *c.* 1960. A workman walks along the walkway between the lime pits. He wears protective leggings. Bags of chemicals, probably lime, are stacked on the right. Pulleys and chains were used to transfer the hides which previously had been carried out by hand, as shown in the previous photograph.

Above: Another picture from the beam house of Harvey's Tannery, *c.* 1960. In this photograph, stacks of hides can be clearly seen. Around this time there weren't sufficient hides coming from the UK and the tannery was importing animal hides from Argentina. Splitting was carried out in the beam house, separating the hides for different uses. Most of the tanned leather went into the shoe trade for sole leather while the rest would be used for upholstery. An advertisement of the same time states, 'The footprints of the wise are made by Harvey's leather, which is trodden underfoot all over the world.'

Left: Tanned hides at Harvey's Tannery, *c.* 1960. A tannery worker with a big pile of hides (at a later stage in the process), perhaps ready for trimming and polishing. The tannery was the biggest employer of male labour in the town and when it suddenly closed in 1972, despite the order books being full, it didn't go down too well with the employees.

The Baronia factory of John Harding & Son, 1895. The clothing factory was built in 1872 making good quality coats, suits and sporting wear for the emerging middle classes. It was the second clothing factory of John Harding & Son of Manchester and it very quickly became the biggest employer of female labour in the town. It was extended in 1888.

One of a series of publicity photographs taken at J.H. Harding's Baronia works in the mid-1930s. This one shows the men's section of the cutting room. The large room was well lit with natural light from the roof windows. Paper templates of the cutting pattern are shown placed on the material prior to cutting by hand. There is no sign of any machinery here.

Opposite above: Another photograph from J.H. Harding's Baronia works in the mid-1930s, showing female staff working on the production of boys' clothing. Sewing machines are much in evidence. Again, natural light is provided by roof windows as well as those in the walls. All are aware of the photographer taking this shot.

Opposite below: A mid-1930s photograph showing a section of the finishing department. Again, it is an all-female staff and J.H. Harding was the biggest employer of female labour in the town at this time. Some of the staff wear pinafores. They sit on low wooden stools and complete the item of clothing by hand sewing.

An aerial view of the J.H. Harding Baronia works, around 1950. The absence of traffic on the roads is striking. In the foreground is the Barony Park with railings. In the lower right-hand corner is the Wood Methodist Chapel and the nissen huts, which, for a short time in the 1950s, were used by the Nantwich Boys' Club before they moved to Birchin Lane.

Right: Nantwich Mill, *c.* 1950. Situated at the lower end of Mill Street, it has stood on this site for centuries. At this time it was used as a store for animal feeds by the local firm of John Boughey. On the top of the frontage in the little wooden housing hung the mill bell used for the mill workers when it was a cotton mill. The bell is now to be seen in Nantwich Museum.

Left: A side view of the same building in the previous photograph, *c.* 1950. The mill is in a state of disrepair and a metal tie-rod can be seen. In the background can be seen some of the cottages on Bower's Row, named after one of the previous mill owners and built for some of the cotton mill workers. These were demolished around 1970. The building on the extreme right was used as a cotton twist warehouse in 1850.

An interior view of Nantwich Mill, *c.* 1950. This is one of the middle floors of the mill. A chute can be seen on the right where the grain would be fed from an upper floor to the mill stones on the floor beneath. Some sacks of animal feed are stored on the floor on the left. The mill was still being used by the firm of John Boughey. There is a feeling of empty spaciousness in this photograph.

6

AGRICULTURE & DAIRY

An early twentieth-century Dobson's milk float. This photograph is thought to show Joe Dobson and his family (from Cronkinson Farm) outside the market hall. They are obviously commemorating some national event as evidenced by the flags, flowers and buttonholes – it just might be the coronation of King George V in 1911, although the photograph could be a later one from the 1920s.

Spencer's milk float in the early 1930s. Horace Spencer of Shrewbridge Road had a milk round in the town in the 1930s. He is standing on the extreme right. His float is thought to be part of the parade for the Annual Cottage Hospital Fête and is seen here promoting the benefits of drinking milk. The boarded-up buildings behind may be on Beam Street, where the bus station is now.

Opposite above: Nantwich Dairy Show, 1932. This photograph was taken in Nantwich market hall. The 56lb cheeses were placed on the floor on straw and there are a surprising number of them in this photograph. Around this time would be the peak in farmhouse Cheshire cheese production. It is thought that the bowler-hatted gentlemen were officials and the person between them is holding a medal with a ribbon.

Opposite below: Judges at Nantwich Dairy Show, 1932. From left to right are Mr Castle from Manchester, clerk to the show, Mr Arnold from Nantwich, Mr A.J. Emberton from Embertons of Crewe, Mr A. Rollings also from Embertons, Miss Nellie Benion from the Cheshire School of Agriculture but representing the Cheshire Cheese Federation, Mr J.H. Williams from P.H. Chesters of Nantwich, Mr S.P. Griffiths from Griffiths of Northwich, and Mr E. Holding from Liptons, Nantwich.

This photograph shows the same girl from the photographs opposite, raking hay. In the distance, a Reaseheath farmhand is on a tractor cutting the hay. No doubt they will be hoping for a few dry days – the war seems a million miles away!

Opposite above: A land army girl at the Cheshire School of Agriculture, Reaseheath, *c.* 1942. Some 1,200 girls were trained here in poultry keeping, animal husbandry and arable farming during the Second World War. They were then sent out to local farms whose regular farmhands had joined the forces. This photograph shows the Women's Hostel at Reaseheath in the background.

Opposite below: Land army girls at Reaseheath, *c.* 1942. In this photograph the land army girls appear to be hoeing among young plants on the estate. The land girls trained at Reaseheath proved to be capable workers where farmers had sometimes been hostile to female labour.

The dairymaid in this picture, from around 1945, is standing next to a wooden butter worker, used to work the butter by removing excess moisture and achieving uniformity from the newly churned butter mass. Behind her is a wooden butter churn and a row of upright cheese presses, which suggests that the equipment could have been used for whey butter as well as for ordinary butter production.

A Cheshire farmhouse dairy scene, Overton Hall, Malpas, *c.* 1950. A young dairymaid stands with a wooden cheese mould with metal liner. Behind her are more empty wooden cheese moulds and upright presses with filled moulds of curd which are being pressed. Several large 56lb cheeses stand on the table in the foreground and the many Cheese Show prize cards indicate the success of the dairy.

Cheshire cheese manufacture at Newhall Dairies, *c.* 1960. Head cheesemaker, Walter Griffiths, and assistant head cheesemaker, Horace Stevenson, are breaking the curd into small pieces by hand during the cheese-making process. Cheese is being made in rectangular 1,000-gallon vats in this factory but the process at this stage still requires much individual handling. There is little sign of mechanisation.

Dairy Crest, Aston, 1983. Some twenty-three years later, on the same premises and with changes of ownership through Unigate to Dairy Crest, Cheshire cheese manufacture finally ceased at Newhall. The photograph commemorates the last Cheshire cheese made there and the beginning of a new (and ill-fated) dawn of Lymeswold production with a sampling of the new cheese. The two gentlemen in the background are Fred Mitchell, head cheesemaker, on the left and Blair Pritchard, factory manager, on the right.

7

SPORT & LEISURE

Nantwich Cricket Club, 1895. This photograph shows players and friends in front of a tent. None of the people are identifiable from existing photographs of Nantwich Cricket Club, but if it is Nantwich then the photograph would probably have been taken at Kingsley Fields, their home ground for around eighty years.

A shooting party, *c.* 1900. This photograph was taken by William Berry outside a local black and white thatched house. It is marked Haughton on the back of the photograph but, unfortunately, the building cannot be identified, although it does appear to be similar to the Nag's Head at Haughton. The men may be local farmers.

Nantwich Town Band, *c.* 1904. From left to right are: T. Sadler junior, S. Parkes, C. Hassall senior, T. Hassall, A. Parkes, W. Hassall, W. Gilbert, J. Benbow, T. Betley, T. Gilbert and T. Sadler senior. As can be seen from the names, there were several members of the Hassall family in the band. They were excellent musicians and had a high reputation. C. Hassall senior was known as 'Old Charles' and the other Hassalls in the photograph were his sons.

Bowlers at the Bowling Green public house, *c.* 1906. The licensee in 1906 was John Hollingworth – he is the man with the stick sitting sixth from the right in the middle row. Immediately behind him is Piggott, who could be George Piggott, licensee of the Crown Hotel and distant relation of the jockey Lester Piggott. Sitting sixth from the left is Archie MacKinnon, the well-known Nantwich artist who became a national figure after painting a picture of the crucifixion in a cave near Campbeltown in Scotland. He settled in Nantwich and had an artist's studio by the river bridge.

The Cheshire Hounds at Poole Hall, 13 February 1908. At this time, Nantwich was a very popular fox-hunting centre for the well-to-do. It was possible to go to a different meet every day of the week in the area, and riders would come here for the season, staying at the Brine Baths Hotel. Poole Hall was a regular meeting place for the hounds, along with Carden Hall, Calveley Hall and Oulton Hall.

Officials and members of Park Road Bowling Club, *c.* 1910. The Bowling Club opened in 1906 as a 'Gentlemen's Bowling Club'. The first two trophies played for were the Laverton and Bradshaw Cups. Maybe these are the ones shown in the photograph. There is also a prize of a case of fish knives. Some of the players employed young boys to hold and pick up their woods, hence their inclusion in the picture.

Nantwich Town Band, *c.* 1919. Surprisingly, there are no members of the Hassall family in this picture. From left to right, back row: A. Glover, T. Allcock, A.E. Adams, W. Heath, W. Sherrat, R. Blagg, C. Heath, H. Carefull (secretary), W. Ormes. Middle row: W. Butler, G. Harrison (bandmaster), W. Case. Front row: C. Heath (senior), W. Sadler, W. Allcock, W. Adams, F. Meachin. The band continued in existence until 1939.

Sid Ward and his Majestic Dance Band, July 1933. Dance bands were popular from the 1930s to the early 1950s, and this local band was just one of several playing regularly in the area. All were amateur musicians and were in demand as dancing became popular, helped by recorded music on 78rpm records and the wireless programmes featuring big bands.

An official photograph taken at the opening of Nantwich open-air swimming pool in 1935. Three girls pose by the cascade, officials stand in the background and at the far deep end there are men on all three diving boards. The man on the highest board appears to be fully clothed!

Above: Winners of the Nantwich Tennis League Tournament, *c.* 1950. The only person positively identified is Mrs Renee Mason, who is sitting second from the right. The photograph was taken by H. Bullock & Son of Crewe. Tennis has been a popular sport in the area with tennis courts in private gardens, at Nantwich Lawn Tennis Club and the municipal courts in the Barony Park.

Left: Local children at the Willows, *c.* 1960. Before the age of foreign holidays, Nantwich children were quite happy to pretend that the banks of the River Weaver were a seaside beach. The very sandy soil at the Willows added to this impression, and many are seen here bathing happily in the shallow water. In the distance is the weir belonging to Nantwich millrace.

8

EDUCATION

Top Infants' Class, Nantwich Council School, Manor Road, 1920. The children in this picture would all be about 7 years old. There were twenty-two boys and ten girls, giving a total of thirty-two in the class. Author Andrew Lamberton attended the same school some thirty years later, when there were forty-eight pupils in his class!

Nantwich and Acton Grammar School preparatory department, either autumn 1920 or early 1921. This photograph was taken in the room belonging to the Primitive Methodist Chapel, Welsh Row, across the road from the old grammar school building nearly opposite Marsh Lane. Apart from the girl sitting on the floor, the other children appear oblivious to the photographer and are engrossed in their schoolwork.

Nantwich and Acton Grammar School preparatory department, c. 1923. This photograph was taken in the corrugated iron building belonging to the school. The teacher on the right is Miss Grant. A lady on the left, probably a teaching assistant, is helping with a spelling lesson on the floor by placing letters on a blanket. The far one reads 'Fanny – in the kitchen'.

Nantwich and Acton Grammar School preparatory department, c. 1923. Taken at the same time as the previous photograph and in the same building, although showing a different class in a separate room. There are twenty-eight children in this picture, considerably more than in the previous ones.

Nantwich Council School, Manor Road, Homewifery top class, c. 1925. As well as their own pupils, young teenagers from other local Council schools would attend here to learn aspects of adult life. Boys would do woodwork and gardening, while the girls would be taught the basics of home-making, including cookery. In this photograph they are learning to wash and iron.

Willaston School, London Road, *c.* 1925. When the school was built in 1900 it was attached to The Grove house – originally the home of the Barker family – on the right in the picture. This building was then used as the headmaster's house. In later years, extensions were added at right angles to the left-hand section of buildings and so this view is now partly obscured. The school was known locally as Willaston College, to differentiate it from Willaston Council School in Crewe Road, Willaston.

Nantwich and Acton Grammar School, *c.* 1925. Building was started on a new grammar school at the far end of Welsh Row around 1914, but was interrupted by the First World War. It wasn't until 1921 that the buildings were completed and the pupils moved from the premises at 108 Welsh Row. The school turned comprehensive in 1977 and is now known as Malbank School and Sixth Form College.

Nantwich and Acton Grammar School Football Team, 1925. This is a good photograph of the First Eleven Football Team for the 1924/25 season and their record is plain for all to see on the coconut mat. The teacher with them is unknown. These were the days of heavy boots and heavy footballs. Two are wearing a different shirt from the others, maybe they were house colours. The school badge is visible on most shirts.

Nantwich and Acton Grammar School, class photograph, c. 1930. The presence of cobblestones in the photograph suggests that this photograph was taken outside the old building further along Welsh Row. Classrooms here were used for years to supplement those in the more modern building. There are twelve girls and fifteen boys and the teacher is wearing his gown, which was a tradition in grammar schools here for some forty years.

Nantwich and Acton Grammar School, class photograph, 1934. All the girls are in gymslips apart from the one in guide uniform. This suggests that there was a definite move around this time towards the adoption of a school uniform. The boys are all wearing similar jackets but they don't look like school blazers. They are, however, all wearing the same tie. The teacher is unknown.

Nantwich and Acton Grammar School, 3rd Nantwich Rangers and Guides, 1934. The girl standing in the back row on the extreme right is also in the previous photograph. Around this time, Scouting and Guiding was becoming popular and several local schools formed their own troops and packs. The hats of the guides help to date this photograph.

9

EVENTS

Recruiting procession in the Square, 1914. A brass band is marching in the crowded square. As some are in uniform, they may be from the town band and were perhaps supplemented by others who are not in uniform. Amid national euphoria and patriotic fervour, many thousands of men volunteered during the early months of August and September 1914. Nantwich was no different from any other market town in providing men for the armed forces at this time.

Float for a local fête, *c.* 1916. The title of the float, 'The Hand that Rocks the Cradle Rules the World' is taken from a poem by W.R. Wallace, written in 1865. The saying became famous in 1916, when it was used as a recurring motif in the film of that year, *Intolerance*. The phrase is in praise of motherhood as the pre-eminent force for change. The float is outside Dr Mathews' house and surgery at No. 50 Welsh Row and the occasion is thought to be the annual Nantwich Cottage Hospital Fête.

The Prince of Wales visiting Nantwich in October 1926. His Royal Highness the Prince of Wales (later to become the Duke of Windsor) is inspecting First World War veterans on parade in the Square. He had just arrived in an open-top car from Chester, accompanied by the Lord Lieutenant of Cheshire, Brigadier-General Sir William Bromley-Davenport. Flags and bunting decorate the streets and shop fronts. Onlookers in an upper window of Stretch & Harlock's shop on the right have a grandstand view.

His Royal Highness the Prince of Wales has just laid a wreath at the War Memorial and is in conversation with Sir William Bromley-Davenport. Crowds stand patiently in the background, being kept in order by two policemen.

The photograph is marked on the back 1926, and it can only be the Prince of Wales' visit to Nantwich in October of that year. Firemen are on parade in front of their two fire engines, one with its ladder extended. Beyond them is a small group of scouts and further on what looks like members of the St John Ambulance Brigade. The shop front of F.W. Woolworth's can be clearly seen on the right. Selo films, as advertised by Grices the Chemist, was the trade name for Ilford photographic films.

The Prince of Wales visiting Nantwich, 1926. After the ceremony on the Square, HRH the Prince of Wales makes his way along Barony Road in an open Rolls-Royce tourer. Crowds line the roadway. John Harding's Baronia works is decorated with flags and bunting and a large banner says 'Baronia workers welcome our Prince'. Note the cloche hats, the fashion of the day.

Rows of Baronia clothing factory employees wait to get a glimpse of the Prince of Wales as he goes past on his way to the Cheshire School of Agriculture at Reaseheath, where he will open a new dairy, women's hostel and farm buildings.

Right: A local hunt meet in the Square, *c.* 1930. Crowds three to four deep line each side of the street to see the horses and hounds of a local hunt, maybe the South Cheshire. The hounds lead the way, surprisingly well-controlled, with the mounted riders following some way behind. On the extreme right is the corner of G.F & A. Brown's wine and spirit merchant's shop, confirming that the photograph was taken in Nantwich Square.

Below: Another local hunt meeting on the Square in the 1930s. It is thought the Delves-Broughtons from Doddington Hall are in the photograph, but they are rather difficult to identify. Top hats were still being worn by some male riders, bowlers by most of the others, and also the occasional trilby. This could be the Cheshire Hunt but there is no sign of the hounds in this shot.

National celebrations marking the coronation of King George V1 in 1937. There was a strong feeling of goodwill towards the Royal Family judging by the decorated streets. This photograph was taken in High Street looking towards the Square, with cars from the era completing the scene. The well-known local clothing shop of Densems can be seen on the right.

Another photograph taken in 1937 of a well-decorated Welsh Row. A Wolseley car stands outside Mrs Heath's haberdashery and toy shop, beyond which is a temperance bar on the corner of First Wood Street. The *Cheshire Observer* office is in Astles, the newsagents shop, on the left.

Royal visit, July 1940. King George VI and Queen Elizabeth make their way by car through the rain-soaked streets of the town, although the weather does not appear to have deterred the crowds. Uniformed soldiers stand to attention as the procession goes past. The picture was taken by local photographer Clifford Kendall.

Nantwich Civic Hall, 1952. At a special ceremonial gathering, Queen Elizabeth II was proclaimed Queen in February 1952. Sir Otho Glover, Chairman of Cheshire County Council, read the proclamation in front of civic dignitaries. Councillor Albert Peake, Chairman of Nantwich Urban District Council, can be seen wearing his chain of office in the background. Note the ceremonial sword on the extreme right.

Coronation Day street party in Prachett's Row, 1953. All over the country, street parties were held to commemorate the coronation of Queen Elizabeth II on 2 June 1953. Most Nantwich streets had a children's outdoor party and Prachett's Row was no exception. The young lady with the fancy hat in the centre foreground is Joan Dale. Immediately behind her is her sister, Muriel Shakeshaft (née Hope), with their mother on her left (the viewer's right). Councillor Albert Peake and his wife are in the background far left.

Re-enactment of the Battle of Nantwich, c. 1978. Each year since 1972, the town has celebrated this battle of 1644 with a re-enactment using members of the Sealed Knot Society. This takes place on the nearest Saturday to 25 January and is known as 'Holly Holy Day', after townsfolk originally celebrated the occasion with sprigs of holly in their hats.

10

TRANSPORT

Horse and carriage at Dorfold Hall, Acton, c. 1895. Around this time Charles Roundell and his wife Julia (née Tomkinson) were living at Dorfold Hall. He was 67 years old in 1895 and the gentleman in the photograph appears to be a good deal younger than that and therefore it is doubtful if it is him. It is difficult to be precise as to the type of carriage this is, although it could be a gig.

Mr and Mrs Thomas Johnson in his homemade motor vehicle, *c*. 1895. Thomas Johnson was a well-known personality in Nantwich. He ran the printing firm of Johnson's of Nantwich (which is still operating) and was responsible for printing James Hall's book on the history of Nantwich. He was an inventor and great innovator. The vehicle in this photograph appears to be a very early motorcycle.

A Bulkeley couple travel in style in 1903 on what appears to be another early motorcycle. The registration number confirms that it was registered in Bristol and is obviously one of the first issues. The basketwork chair as part of the sidecar is unusual and the wheels are almost as big as bicycle wheels. Note the carbide lamp on the front.

Wrenbury Station, *c.* 1910. On the left, outside the Salamanca Hotel, is a donkey cart with young passengers. In front of the station building is a pony and trap and two more horse carriages wait on the right. Together with the horse and the railway, the bicycle in the picture provides a third means of transport.

A tranquil view of Wellington Road, *c.* 1910. On the left are two young boys with a bicycle. In the distance is possibly a stationary horse and cart and, coming towards the viewer, is another horse-drawn vehicle. This was a regular route from the Brine Baths Hotel to Nantwich Station and this could well have come from the Hotel with passengers and luggage. On the right is a motionless horse with mounted rider. He will need to move out of the way!

A nice photograph of a group of people around a horse-drawn brake, *c.* 1910. This provided transport for twelve people sitting in two rows and facing each other – in this picture it seems to be mostly ladies. Two men in the foreground are holding modern bicycles.

Mr and Mrs Laverton outside Stapeley Grange, *c.* 1910. Mr Walter Laverton was a retired cotton merchant who lived in Wellington Road, Nantwich and was perhaps visiting Stapeley Grange in his new car. It is certainly the front of Stapeley Grange, and in 1910 Charles Weaver was living there with his wife and daughter, Cynthia. Many years later, Cynthia married a Mr Zur Nedden, and, when she died, left her fortune to the RSPCA, who now have an animal hospital on the site.

Chetwood's Garage, Crewe Road End, *c.* 1920. Around this time, William Chetwood expanded his business in Hospital Street with the purchase of the site. He was able to trade on the commercial success of the Ford Motor Company and probably all the vehicles in this photograph are Ford cars. There is a petrol pump in the middle of the photo. The large spaniel in the car on the right steals the scene.

A Leyland milk tanker belonging to United Dairies, *c.* 1935. Perhaps it was going to the nearest United Dairies depot, the milk bottling plant at Calveley. This depot closed in the late 1960s and has been replaced with a modern housing estate. Note the starting handle on the front of the lorry. As this is an intensive area for milk production, tankers were a familiar sight.

Watson's Garage, Welsh Row, *c.* 1965. This stood where King's Court houses now stand. Earlier tenants were Cooke's and Moore & Creighton. The garage was an agent for Standard and Triumph cars and was RAC recommended. It also had three petrol pumps selling National petrol. There is a Triumph Herald car parked outside and on the right is a Standard Ten van. Note also the portable ladders in the foreground.

Cyclists outside Watson's Garage, *c.* 1965. This photograph is taken looking in the opposite direction along Welsh Row, away from the town. The young cyclists are obviously just coming out of Nantwich and Acton Grammar School and heading home. There is another Triumph Herald parked outside the garage – this one in two-tone colours. Note the overhanging trees from the garden of Townsend House.

11

DODDINGTON

Wanda and Julian Socha at the Polish Resettlement Camp, Doddington, in the 1950s. Between 1946 and 1960, part of the Doddington Hall Estate, near Nantwich, was home to a thriving Polish community housed at a resettlement camp for displaced persons. The camp was one of many set up by the Government to house members of the Polish armed services and their families, who were unable to return home after fighting alongside the British in the Second World War.

Stan Was and some of his extended family outside one of the huts, *c.* 1958. Despite the hardships of camp life, the residents worked hard to turn the huts into well-maintained and happy homes. There was no running water in the huts and so water for drinking, cooking and washing up had to be fetched in buckets. There were two communal wash-houses and shower blocks, and in the early days there was a communal kitchen.

The altar in the church at the camp. Most of the residents of the camp were Catholic and their faith and tradition were very important to them. A Catholic church was soon set up in one of the huts and it had its own Polish priest. Over the years the church was the venue for numerous weddings, baptisms and funerals. There was no cemetery and so the deceased of the camp were buried in the graveyard of Wybunbury church.

Children, parents and teachers pose for a photograph outside the camp school, 1948. It didn't take long for a school to be established so that primary education could be provided at the camp. The headmaster was Mr Pialucha and the teachers included Mr Czerski and Mr Czaplinski. There was also an English teacher called Miss Pugsly. As their English improved, some of the children attended local primary schools including Bridgemere, Wybunbury and St Anne's in Nantwich, before continuing into secondary education.

Dedication of one of the Corpus Christi altars in the 1950s. Every year, in May or June, the camp celebrated the feast of Corpus Christi with prayers and a procession. Four special open-air altars were erected around the camp and the procession would stop at each one for prayers. The day was very special and involved the whole community in celebration and worship.

Above: The Corpus Christi procession leaving the church. Mr Smolinski, the camp's boiler man, carries the cross at the head of the procession on the way to the first altar. Following him are a group of children and behind them the canopy covering the Blessed Sacrament can just be seen. The top of the tower housing the church bell is just visible to the left of the photograph behind the church.

Left: Helen and Jerzy Bialozorski with their daughter Barbara at The Bluebell Wood, Doddington. As the 1950s progressed, more and more people from the camp found jobs in the surrounding towns and cities and people gradually started to move out of the camp and into houses. The camp closed in 1960, when the last remaining families were allocated council housing in Crewe. Like many others who lived at the camp as children, Barbara has happy memories of growing up in a safe and secure environment, surrounded by beautiful countryside.

Children making their First Holy Communion at the camp church in the late 1950s. The priest is Father Wladysellaw Puchalski and the children include Zdzisia Zakrzewska, Wanda Banas, Staszek Zakrzewski, Basia Kosarew, Michalina Gorajewska and Teresa Kolociew.

A photograph before setting off for carol singing around the camp, 1955. A group of children pose for a photograph around the crib with their teacher, Mr Czerski. The crib and the stars will be carried around the camp as they sing the carols. In keeping with Polish tradition, children received presents not only on Christmas Day but also on the feast of St Nicholas on 6 December.

The wedding of Zosia and Edward Puchalski at Doddington, 1950s. They had a traditional Polish wedding with seven bridesmaids and seven groomsmen. Those pictured include Stasia Bielec, Jurek Jermacz, Tadek Wisniewski, Pani Wisniewska, St Mierzwinski, Marysia (Pitolcio), Danusia Kaszycka, Marysia Czestochowska, Mirek Stranc, Heniek Rojek, Marjan Rojek and Konstanty Ancuta.

12

RELIGION

Reverend Andrew Chater, *c.* 1870. The Revd Chater was rector at St Mary's parish church Nantwich from 1846 until his death at the age of 57 in 1872. He played a prominent role during the cholera epidemic in the town in 1849 in attending the poor and sick and also chairing the Local Board of Health, which was set up to improve the town's sanitation and water supply. He also oversaw the major restoration of the church under Sir Gilbert Scott.

Left: Reverend Charles Jackson, *c.* 1905. The Revd Jackson was rector at St Mary's parish church Nantwich from 1894 to 1910. He was a fine scholar and distinguished preacher. He did great work in improving and enlarging the Market Street School. Owing to his Oxford connections, he brought many distinguished preachers into the town and was himself a fine lecturer. He left to take up a position in the Durham diocese in 1910.

Below: Interior of St Mary's Church, Nantwich, *c.* 1920. Looking towards the chancel, this view does not look much different from today. The gates at the rood screen are closed. The floor was lowered 2ft and the wooden pews were installed during the Sir Gilbert Scott restoration of 1855-61. The font on the right is made of Caen stone and is not particularly old.

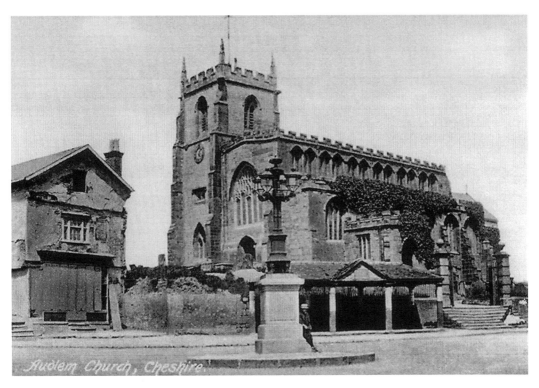

St James's Church, Audlem, *c.* 1910. The church dates from the thirteenth century, with nineteenth-century additions. It stands in a prominent position on a mound in the centre of the village. The ivy has since been removed from the exterior. The building to the left appears in a dilapidated condition and the main shop window is boarded up. The butter market in front of the church still stands today.

St Margaret's Church, Wrenbury, *c.* 1925. This is an early sixteenth-century building with eighteenth- and nineteenth-century additions. It is made of red sandstone and has battlemented parapets and a square tower. The building on the left was evidently the vicarage. It is now privately owned and called Birchwood House.

St Mary's Church, Nantwich, *c.* 1930. The north transept of the church can be clearly seen on the right. The Sir Gilbert Scott restoration raised the roofs of both North and South transepts to their present height around 1855. Access to the bell-ringing chamber is via a door on the west side of the North transept. Since 1875, the church vestry has been situated internally here.

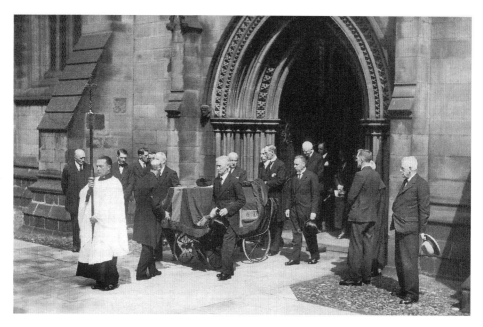

Funeral at St Mary's, Nantwich, *c.* 1935. Unfortunately nothing is known about this photograph but it is interesting in that it shows the bier used for transporting coffins to and from the church. The mourning party are emerging from the west door of the church into bright sunlight. It is interesting to see the black silk top hats worn by the funeral party. The homburg hat held by the gentleman on the right helps to date this picture.

Unitarian Chapel, off Hospital Street, Nantwich, *c.* 1957. This chapel was built in 1726 and served a small Unitarian congregation for almost 250 years until its demolition in 1970. Its most famous minister was Joseph Priestley, the discoverer of oxygen, who preached and taught at a school here from 1758 to 1761. His name is commemorated in Priestley Court, which is now built on this site.

St Mary's parish church choir at RAF Hack Green, *c.* 1958. A service at Hack Green was held here with the Bishop of Stockport. From left to right, standing: -?-, Kenneth Densem, Marshall Hodgkinson, John Clewlow, the Revd Eric Southwell (rector of St Mary's), Harry Moulton, Harold Kirkham (organist), Michael Johnson, David Moseley. Seated in the middle is the Bishop of Stockport, to his right the RAF chaplain and to each side the commanding officers.

Left: A Rolls-Royce in St Mary's parish church, Nantwich, 1977. This Rolls-Royce motor car was the centrepiece of the Harvest Festival celebrations at St Mary's parish church in 1977. It was the brainchild of the Revd Jim Richardson, rector of St Mary's, and it made the national press in that year. Apparently, there was some difficulty in manoeuvring the car down the steps at the west end of the church. The Revd Jim Richardson is on the left, with a representative from Rolls-Royce behind. On the right at the front is the Revd Harold Hewitt.

Below: The Baptist chapel, Market Street, 1972. This chapel was built in 1873 with seating for 350 people. It replaced the earlier, smaller chapel in Barker Street. At that time its congregation was just forty-two people. By 1966, it had become infected with dry rot and was in poor condition. It was demolished in July 1981, the only remaining part being the Victorian hall behind. This was redeveloped to become the new Market Street church in 1986.

13

HEALTH

Acton Red Cross Hospital, *c.* 1916. A group of men and women dressed up as pierrots sit in the snow outside Acton Village Hall. Cards are held which spell out the name of the village followed by question marks. This may have been a fundraising event for the Red Cross Hospital. Acton Village Hall was one of three VAD (Voluntary Aid Detachment) Hospitals in the Nantwich Division of the Red Cross Society and was used as a convalescent hospital for wounded soldiers during the First World War.

The Dowery Red Cross Hospital, *c.* 1916. The Dowery in Barker Street was another of the Red Cross Hospitals in the Nantwich Division used for convalescing soldiers. The men are all patients and are wearing the same type of jacket with large white lapels. One, in a wheelchair, holds a dog, the other wheelchair is of a basket-type with a front steering handle, rather like a bath chair.

Another photograph of convalescing soldiers at the Dowery, *c.* 1918. Again all of the men are wearing the same overalls but the style of dress indicates a slightly later date than the previous photograph. They are sitting in the sunshine enjoying the pleasant surroundings of the garden leading down to the River Weaver, which at this point was the headrace to Nantwich Mill.

Cheerbrook Hospital at Stapeley House, *c.* 1918. Another Red Cross Hospital was at Stapeley House and known at the time as Cheerbrook Hospital. Although the Christie-Miller family owned the house, it was under the patronage of Baroness Schroeder from Rookery Hall. Dr Wyncoll from Willaston sits among the convalescing soldiers and Red Cross nurses.

Red Cross nurses outside Stapeley House, *c.* 1944. Stapeley House was again used as a Red Cross Hospital for convalescent soldiers in the Second World War. There are sixty nurses in this photograph and they would probably have worked in various Red Cross hospitals in the area. Out of the sixty, only two can currently be identified. Fifth from the left in the front row is Dora Green, and third from the left in the third row from the back is Muriel Gilford.

Nantwich Union Workhouse, *c.* 1920. The building at the rear on the right is the workhouse, originally built on the Barony in 1780. It became known as the Nantwich Union Workhouse in 1837, when it served over eighty-six parishes and townships in the county. Later buildings were added, as can be seen in the foreground. It ceased to be a workhouse in 1930 and became the Barony Hospital, surviving in various forms until its closure in 1994.

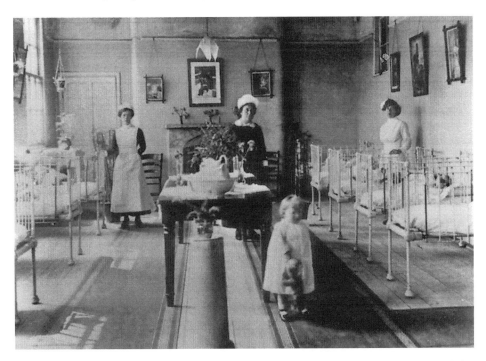

Nantwich Union Workhouse, *c.* 1920. This is the interior of the children's dormitory of the workhouse. It is known that a childrens home and school were built in 1880 to accommodate sixty children, and this may be part of that building. Two nurses and a sister, together with a child, pose for the photographer.

Nursing staff and child at Nantwich Union Workhouse, *c.* 1920. This looks like two senior and two junior nurses, with the senior nurses sitting down. They wear dark blouses with starched cuffs and a curious ruff-like collar. The little girl seems a picture of health. Note the boots, typical of the period. The iron gate on the right and flagged floor suggest a workhouse environment.

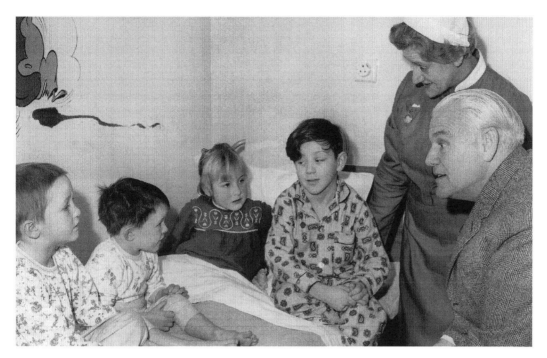

Wing Commander Grant-Ferris visits children at Nantwich Cottage Hospital, c. 1963. This photograph is taken from Miss Mary Duncalf's photograph album. She was the matron at the Cottage Hospital for many years and she can be seen in the background. Robert Grant-Ferris was the Member of Parliament for the Nantwich constituency from 1955 to 1974.

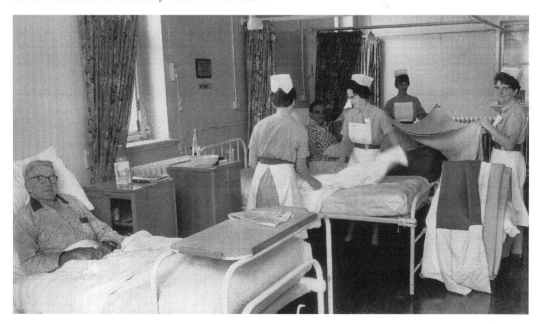

The men's ward, Nantwich Cottage Hospital, c. 1963. Another photograph taken from Miss Duncalf's photograph album. Nurses are changing the sheets on an unoccupied bed. Men and women in those days occupied separate wards. It would be unusual nowadays to have so many nurses together.

Nantwich Cottage Hospital, *c.* 1969. The Cottage Hospital is regarded with much affection by Nantwich residents and it served the local community well from its foundation in 1911 until its closure around 1972. There was a men's ward, a women's ward and a children's ward, with a total of twenty-two beds. In the 1950s, operations were carried out by Doctors Knowles and Lipscombe. Dr Knowles was the surgeon and Dr Lipscombe the anaesthetist.

14

PERSONALITIES

Nantwich Volunteer Fire Brigade, 1870. From left to right, back row: J. Pooley, W. Johnson, J. Moore Johnson, A. Boyer, R. Roberts, T. Knight, W. Green. Front row: R. Lloyd, W. Howell, J. Steventon, J.R. Palmer, C. Laxton, J. Walley, W. Prince, T. Daniels, J. Heywood, T. Parry, H. Gentry, G. Foden. Charles Laxton (with the brass helmet) was the Captain and he was also superintendent of the police for Nantwich. The Volunteer Fire Brigade was formed in 1868 after a disastrous fire on Snow Hill.

Above: Nantwich Volunteer Fire Brigade, 1889. From left to right, back row: W. Pierce, T. Cartlidge, E. Bayliss, F. Barnett, W. Johnson, J. Gentry, H. Gentry. Front row: E. Lloyd, L. Carrington, G. Harding, G. Foden, J.C. Gilbert, H.T. Johnson, C. Hampson. By this time, the brigade had a station next door to the Council fire brigade in Market Street and there was intense rivalry between the two brigades.

Left: The Bell Family, *c.* 1895. Pictured from left to right are Ellen White Bell, Rupert, William, Evelyn, Percy and Florence. Ellen White Bell held strong opinions against the compulsory vaccination of children against smallpox during the latter part of the nineteenth century, and she refused to have her six children vaccinated, resulting in her husband being sent to gaol and her having to raise the family single-handedly. None of them contracted the disease, thus vindicating her strong views. She died, however, comparatively young at the age of 56.

Right: Herbert H. St John Jones with his sister, Emily, in 1902. Herbert was a well-known animal painter and lived at this time with his sister at No. 13 Shrewbridge Road. When this photograph was taken in 1902 he was 30 years old and had already earned a reputation as a local artist. His particular interest was drawing and painting horses and he had many commissions from well-to do families. He also painted local scenes of the town at the turn of the century, several of which are on display in Nantwich Museum.

Below: Mr Nicholson's family of Cholmondeley and South Africa, staying at The Grove, *c.* 1910. The Grove around this time had become the headmaster's house belonging to Willaston School and this family were perhaps guests of the then headmaster, Henry Lang Jones. His predecessor, Guy Lewis, had resigned the headship in 1905 and had accepted a job in South Africa. Whether this is a coincidence or not, we may never know. The photograph is taken in the garden of The Grove.

Left: Mr Mathias, Master of Nantwich Union Workhouse, *c.* 1911. In that year, at the age of 40, William Morgan Mathias was head of an institution of 194 adults and seventy-eight children. His wife, Lucy, was matron. They had a small team of eight assistants including a porter, a cook, a laundress, a workhouse assistant, a labour master, a male and a female industrial trainer, and an assistant matron. The rest of the adults were classed as inmates and the children as being at school.

Below: The wedding of Mr George Egerton and Miss Harding, 1911. This is a really nice photograph of a Nantwich wedding in the Edwardian era. The men wear top hats and the ladies are in their finest dresses and hats. The bride sits in the front middle, with her husband, top hat in hand, standing behind her. The bridesmaid to the right of the bride is Mrs Taylor and on her left are Mr and Mrs Henry Harding, probably the bride's parents. On the extreme right is the Revd Pratt. The bridesmaid on the left of the bride is Mrs Stanley Harding.

Above: Apprentices and delivery boys of P.H. Chesters', *c.* 1920. The stables were at the rear of his wholesale premises in Pepper Street, where some twenty-one horses were kept. His staff of young men were drawn mainly from Wesleyan families and several were Sunday school teachers. These young men were called Philip Chesters' disciples when they marched two-by-two, twice every Sunday, to the Methodist Chapel in Hospital Street and sat side by side in a long pew under the gallery.

Right: Olive Morris, Nantwich Rose Queen, *c.* 1920. There is no information regarding this young lady other than her name. Nantwich does, however, have a good record in producing beauty queens, with Yvonne Ormes crowned Miss United Kingdom in 1970, and Carolyn Moore crowned Miss Great Britain later that decade. Olive's crown is now on display in Nantwich Museum.

Nantwich Beam Heath Trustees, 1919. From left to right, back row: Wilkinson, T. Barlow, T.V. Thistlewaite, H.T. Johnson, C.S.P. Brooke, L. Vaughan, H. Bebbington, J.C. Gilbert, W.H. Edwards. Front row: R. Wright, W.E. Walker, A. Furnival, E.G. Steventon, A.N. Hornby, H. Knowles, J.D. Munro. Some well-known Nantwich figures are among this group, including Albert Hornby, the famous cricketer, and Dr John Douglas Ross Munro, a local practitioner from Kiltearn House, Hospital Street. Also shown are Harry Johnson, printer and Captain of the Volunteer Fire Brigade, and standing next to him Thomas Thistlethwaite, Captain of the Council Fire Brigade, who lived at The Gables, Beam Street.

Mr Herbert Halfpenny, head gardener of the Brine Baths Hotel, *c.* 1923.
Mr Halfpenny was head gardener at the hotel for more than twenty years.
He was highly thought of by his employers and respected by his own staff,
being firm but fair. He is seen here in the rose garden, thought to have one
of the best displays of roses in south Cheshire. The hotel estate had extensive
parkland with many mature trees. There was also a walled kitchen garden,
fruit orchards, herbaceous borders and greenhouses, including an orchid
glasshouse, all of which came under his responsibility. He always wore a
hessian apron, as seen in the photograph.

William Berry, Nantwich photographer, in 1924. William took over the photography business of Henry Bowker at No. 21 Churchyardside some time between 1890 and 1896. He also expanded into picture framing as well. Nantwich people will have family portraits taken by him and it is good to see the face behind the camera.

Nantwich Urban District Council officials, *c.* 1952. Councillor Albert Peake, Chairman of the Council, stands wearing his chain of office. On the left is Tudor Evans, long-serving clerk to the Council. At the time, the Council consisted of a chairman, vice chairman, three representatives each from the Barony ward, Weaver ward, Wellington ward and Willaston ward, plus clerk and deputy clerk. The clerk's duties also included those of Rating Officer and Financial Officer. The Council served a population of over 8,000 at that time.

Richard Dimbleby from the BBC radio programme 'Down Your Way' visits Nantwich around 1954. Mr Dimbleby, by this time, was a national figure, having commentated the previous year at the televised Queen's coronation. The popular radio programme was broadcast on a Sunday afternoon on the Home Service. He visited a Nantwich clothing factory, probably Harding's Baronia clothing factory, and spoke to some employees asking them about their work and for their choice of a piece of music.

Left: Cynthia Zur Nedden, *c.* 1955. Cynthia Zur Nedden (*née* Weaver), was born into a privileged lifestyle at Stapeley Grange in 1908. During the Second World War, she undertook the duties of billeting officer for Liverpool evacuees. She married in 1947 and after her husband's death in 1975 devoted her life to the care of sick animals and birds. On her death, she bequeathed Stapeley Grange to the RSPCA to provide an animal home and sanctuary.

Below: Artist Dorothy Bradford in her studio. Dorothy has exhibited her paintings worldwide and examples of her work are in collections in America, Australia, South Africa and other countries. Her paintings are mainly of music and dance and reflect a fluidity that is quite unique. She was associated with Nantwich Museum for several years and held regular exhibitions in the Millennium Gallery. Sadly, she died in 2008, aged 90, but she is remembered with much affection by Nantwich townsfolk and her work is still much sought after.

If you enjoyed this book, you may also be interested in ...

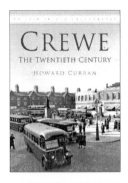

Crewe: The Twentieth Century
HOWARD CURRAN

Illustrated with over 200 archive images, this collection traces the changes and developments that have taken place in Crewe during the twentieth century. The book features many different aspects, from the building of the magnificent Municipal Buildings to the changes on the Market Square. The effects of two world wars upon Crewe and its revival afterwards is also documented.

978 0 7524 6450 3

Merseyside War Years Then & Now
DANIEL K. LONGMAN, COLOUR PHOTOGRAPHY BY TONY SHERRATT

Featuring forty-five vistas of bomb-damaged suburbia and city centre carnage alongside forty-five photographs of the area as it is today, *Merseyside War Years: Then & Now* sensitively documents the changes and developments that have taken place in Merseyside since those dark days of war, demonstrating both architectural progress and Britain's resilience and in the face of adversity.

978 0 7524 6352 0

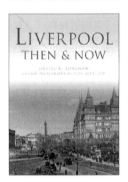

Liverpool Then & Now
DANIEL K. LONGMAN, COLOUR PHOTOGRAPHY BY PETER GOODBODY

Contrasting forty-five archive images with full-colour modern photographs, *Liverpool Then & Now* compares the fashionable man about town to his modern counterparts, and workers of yesteryear with today's trades-people. As well as delighting tourists, it will provide present occupants with a glimpse of how the city used to be, in addition to awakening nostalgic memories for those who used to live or work here.

978 0 7524 5740 6

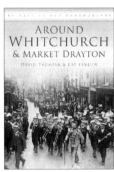

Around Whitchurch & Market Drayton
DAVID TRUMPER & RAY FARLOW

Shropshire historian and author David Trumper has teamed up with Ray Farlow, Shropshire postcard collector extraordinaire, for a feast of photographs that illustrate the bygone days of Whitchurch and Market Drayton. The smaller neighbouring settlements of Newport, Prees, Whixhall, Hodnet, Hawkstone and many others are also featured.

978 0 7509 4671 1

Visit our website and discover thousands of other History Press books.
www.thehistorypress.co.uk